Power From the Sun

Focus: Energy

Meredith Costain

The sun is very big and hot. It is also very powerful.

We get heat from the sun.
The heat from the sun
helps keep us warm.

We get light from the sun.
The light from the sun
helps plants to grow.

We can collect the heat and light from the sun to make power. Power from the sun is called solar power. People use solar power in many ways.

Some people use solar
power to heat water
for their homes. They
put solar panels
on their roofs.
The solar panels
collect heat
from the sun.

Some people use solar power to make their cars go. Solar cars are small and light. They can only travel slowly, but they can go a long way.

Some traffic lights use solar power. Some calculators use solar power. Solar power is cheap and clean. People are learning to use solar power more and more.

Index